Prairie Madness

KATHERINE HOERTH

NDSU NORTH DAKOTA STATE UNIVERSITY PRESS

Poetry of the Plains & Prairies
Volume 6

NDSU NORTH DAKOTA STATE UNIVERSITY PRESS
Dept. 2360, P.O. Box 6050, Fargo, ND 58108-6050
www.ndsupress.org

PRAIRIE MADNESS
By Katherine Hoerth

First Edition

Cover design by Jamie Trosen
Interior design by Deb Tanner

Letterpress printing and assembly by Sam Anderson, Sarah Beck, Tori Layne Eiss, N.J. Hansen, Tatum L. Hoff, Jack T. Monson, Ryan Pedersen, Hannah-Ruth Slater, Erin L. Tamillo, and Kyle Vanderburg, with assistance from Allan Burke, Suzzanne Kelley, and Oliver West Sime.

International Standard Book Number: 978-1-946163-46-2

Printed on site at The Hunter Times (Bonanzaville, West Fargo) and The Braddock News Letterpress Museum, North Dakota, USA

The production of *Prairie Madness* is a collaboration of The Hunter Times, The Braddock News Letterpress Museum, NDSU Press, and the fall 2021 Introduction to Publishing class at NDSU.

CONTENTS

Prairie Madness

West Omaha, 2020

The scent of weeping pine trees fills the air.
Instead of crow caws, drill songs ride the wind.
An avenue named Rosewood copperheads
through a neighborhood, suburbia.

The houses grow like stalks in rows, each one
planted carefully, a verdant promise
of tomorrow, reaching toward the blue
Nebraska sky, the openness of it.

How full of gold it feels today: the morning
sunshine bathing all the roofs in butter,
the gold of rings on every finger here,
its history of grain and humble farmers

with their forlorn wives out on the plains,
the harvest and the emptiness that follows.
I'm standing in the middle of it all
staring out my window at the neighbor

jogging past, her hair like mine, the hue
of cornsilk, wheat, a field of grain, our bodies—
all of us in rows of loneliness
driven to madness by the prairie wind.

My Grandma Creates the Earth

At school, I learned the earth was made from dust
and gas leftover from the sun's creation.
It scraped together pieces of itself
and formed a feast of oceans, land, and life.

But none of this made any sense to me—
I'd studied the geography of worry
on the pages of my mother's face,
the tilted axis of her head, a bend
of frown, a river bed around her eyes,
the canyons of her forehead as she'd find
once again more month than dollars
tucked inside the somber cavern of her purse.

I'd come to understand that folks like us
made do with what they had inside their pantries:
scraping the empty peanut butter jar,
mouthfuls of stale bread, saltines with ketchup.
But how could something beautiful be born
of scraps, of what another threw away?

One autumn dusk, my grandma came to visit
on the last day of September, filled
the kitchen with her presence and the bustling
sounds of cooking—whisk on pan, a hiss
and cackling of oil, a bang of pots.
She emptied out the sack of flour,
cracked expired eggs into a bowl. She poured
a swig of sour milk and toasted bread butts,
declared the miracle of Sunday supper,
created from the nothing of the cupboard.

Pancakes rolled, a gold expanse of prairie,
a hill of butter, rivering with syrup,
fluffy clouds of eggs, plateau of toast
smeared with sanguine jelly. Grandma gazed
at my hungry eyes, my mother's smile
as she came home from work to find this feast.
Grandma sat down at the table, sighed
said grace, and knew that it was good.

Paloma Wings

I wondered why maxi pads have wings,
and what the use of wings are
if all they do is hold you in place.

As a kid, I imagined a flock of them,
of maxi pads,
taking to the clouds like startled palomas,

outstretching their white wings
and using them to get as far from me
as possible at that time of the month.

I thought that wings
were only used to fly away—
to touch the sky like Icarus,

who never had to wear a maxi pad.
Who would ever want to be grounded
in such a place, the delta of a river,

to collect the flotsam left behind
from the wreck of another month?
Because when you're thirteen,

you learn there's nothing worse
than yourself, a girl,
the red red red of you.

Pluto's Not a Planet Anymore

As a girl, in science class, you learned
somewhere in the emptiness of space
a planet lurked in darkness, orbiting
the sun some billions of miles away,
world-sized, dominating gravity
within its neighborhood, the nether reaches
of the solar system with its moon.
Its existence was a fact that you
could look up in your textbook or recite
when your third-grade teacher called on you.

Its name was Pluto like the Roman ruler
of the underworld, the one who kidnapped
Proserpina as a girl when youth was blooming
from her body, like it bloomed from yours,
like crocus, violet, lily, larkspur, rose
in an April meadow. She was so lovely
that she caught his eye. She'd wandered off
too far away, alone. A god, like Pluto,
can't help himself, so what did she expect?
He took her straight to hell to be his queen.
It hung above your head, that shadowed planet,
Pluto, out of sight but in your mind,
its umbra casting darkness over everything,
the knowledge somewhere in the night sky, evil
lurks in waiting for the moment springtide
flashes from your lips, a blooming smile.

You spent your childhood believing this:
a myth, a story, or a lie engrained
within your brain. You learned to fear his presence.
You learned that you were insignificant,
a girl who's caught within the gravity
of his embrace, a power simply greater
than you'd ever be. So you held back
the floodgates of your beauty, spoke in whispers,
not the roaring winds of March, the thunder
of April, the boldness of a wild prairie
in full bloom in May. But there was never
a reason on this earth to make yourself
small. Today, the scientists rewrite
the facts and tell us Pluto's just a rock
that can't clear a path around the sun.
It's lifeless, insignificant, a stone—
but an afterthought within the story of our galaxy.
But you contain

A universe of life within your body,
lush and thriving, even giving life.

So who's the god and who's the goddess now?
But they're everywhere, those timid girls,
afraid to step beyond the bounds in fear
because a shadow might sweep in and carry
them away into some underworld.

You want to tell them, Girls, it's just a myth.
For years, we had the facts all wrong, it seems.
Lift up your voice and sing your goddess song.

Bloom, oh millions of Proserpinas.
You have nothing left to fear.
Pluto's not a planet anymore.

Beefmaster

Languidly, they breathe in our exhaust
as they nibble on Bermuda grass,
chomping through the afternoon, their tails

swatting gadflies as they browse. These cows
glance over their shoulders, their black eyes
as deep as history, as dark as myth.

Nothing scares these heifers anymore—
they've seen it all: the plumes of dusky smoke
scented with hickory and notes of brisket,

the darkness of the dust beneath their hooves,
the hunger and the gentleness of gods.
Their stomachs urge their grazing as the sun

gazes from its throne above the clouds.
In a field nearby, the sorghum hums
its song of flourishing as it receives

a dusting from above, the only snow
that falls this time of year out on the plains.
They'll drink it in with sips of morning dew.

The gulf wind stirs the heifers as they wait
for fate, like Io, just a red-haired belle
bred to be devoured by the heavens.

Daughter of Brush Country

Teach her tongue how to roll the names of flowers
tickling her toes, the lantana, nightshade,
primrose. Crown her ebony curls with willow.
Teach her the word for

beauty. Show her summers were meant for sipping
raspas in the shade of mesquites, sun a
mango color turning chamoy by evening.
Teach her the word for

joy. Then let her listen to chachalaca
songs at dusk, the chants of cicadas, chanclas
rapping on caliche, the mix of lenguas.
Teach her the word for

harmony. Now make her see her reflection
in the mirror, see her own birthplace, gaze at
this flat vale, viridian river, Eden.
Teach her the word for home.

Lupinus Texensis

In spring, a striptease of blue petals
fills the vistas. I, delicate,

helpless, harmless, a toothless pup—
bare naked petals, violet lacunas,

perky clusters of pink about to burst
with sweetness.

You might witness the coming of bees,
monarchs, men,

thinking such loveliness exists for them.
But,

in the end, they all taste of me
and wear my mist of pollen.

I always get what I want.
What they don't know—beyond this pretty face,

I am wolf. Not your garden flower.
I bloom where the sun pleases me most,

where the rain tastes the sweetest,
where my roots curl like toes in splendor

as west winds rustle the petals.
Toothed with beauty, I flourish,

the wildflower everybody loves.

Her Golden Goose

Such a gosling is a fragile thing:
emerging from a golden egg, blood-streaked
and alabaster, tail feathers slicked
with sheen, its budding beak a point of pleasure.

Flecked with shell, it still belonged to her
and her alone, a quiet fluttering
within her skin, a sunrise in her darkness,
a breath of burning air that smelled of summer.

It was hers then it belonged to someone
else once downy fluff turned into feathers
and feathers into sky. It had a name
she only whispered to herself—the softness

but a memory of adolescence.
Some nights, her fingers touch that velvet still,
the part of her that once could make her bedroom
shadows dance before it flew away.

She calls it back. Most seasons, though,
her golden goose is continents away.
But sometimes, it can hear her midnight calls, c
omes home to roost with her nest of flesh.

Prairie Verbena

February 2021

No one thought a freeze would come this late—
least of all, verbena blossoms, young
and too naïve to know that February
is a liar with a silver tongue.

A couple balmy afternoons, the warm
tongue of sunshine, dulcet trill of purple martins
blasting like a love song through a bedroom
window, invited every bloom to come
and dance. The soft breeze whispered promises
of a gentle spring, an everlasting summer
filled with warm nights and the pattering
of raindrops—all the things a sweet verbena
needs to thrive. And so, the wildflower
peeked her head up from the earth and opened
the bud, unfurled those petals to the sky

that turned to slate, encased her face in ice,
and smothered her in snow. Verbena blossom,
now the color of a nasty bruise,
limp and shorn, will never hold her head
so high again. A victim of the times

that bloomed too fast, this prairie wildflower—
like a girl, yes always, like a girl.

Sunrise, Chalco Hills

When did you start believing in the sky,
its openness, its emptiness, its splendor
at dawn? It cups this swathe of wilderness
in its hands, ignites the scintillas of dew
with a sunray like a fingertip
extended from the fuchsia clouds above.
The chorus of a flock of warblers fills
this cathedral made of wind and dirt
as elm trees dance, entranced by morning's song.
This miracle, as daily as a perfect
café de olla held against your lips
convinces most that holiness exists
past the horizon, always out of reach.

You've believed this story all your life.
At eight, a babel of construction rips
the prairie open once again. A mower
roars. A dump truck revs its engine loud.
Bulldozers sing the ancient song of progress
to the applause of snapping buckeye bark.
A coyote slinks away, retreats
into the depths of Eden in the distance.
He watches in the shadow of our towers
and our walls, our roads that wind in circles
as we make the same mistakes again.
You hear a mournful howl. You say a prayer.

What Cassandra Knew

She grasped her auburn locks of hair and screamed.
Centuries ago, the world ignored
her prophecies. No one believed that Troy
could turn into a world of ash and bone.
Was it because the lips that carved those words
were supple? Because her voice reminded them
of the lilting of a thrush's song,
rising at the end of every sentence?
Did she squeak? Or screech? Sound shrill?
Did everything she say seem like a question,
not an answer, warning, or the truth?
Maybe she uttered "like" too many times.
But every word flung from her tongue came true.
She watched the ramparts burn, her kingdom fall.
What good is prophecy when you're a woman?

Cassandra, I can feel the flames today
as flare stacks fill the sky like blazing stars.
Cassandra, no one's listening again.
Cassandra, climates change, but man does not.
Cassandra, I am pulling out my hair.

Katy Prairie, May

The prairie knows her time on earth is short—
slips into something slinky every spring

in bright pastels that hint of innocence—
the baby pink of evening primrose, yellow

of wild Susans, coreopsis, sun,
the pale purple of verbena blooms.

She flips her gaudy skirts and giggles
birdsong, frog song, crickets chirping loud

above the city's thump that almost drowns
her desperation out. She smells of sweet

perfume, magnolia and beebalm breathed.
But dandelions keep on turning white.

Cicadas husk on bark. The bluebonnets
have all faded out by now. It's May. The time

is running out for her, for him, for all
who long to kiss amongst the lightning bugs.

It's last call at the bar on Sunday night.
In this pastel ruse of May, she paints

herself one final time the hue of spring.
Come nestle in this grove of loveliness.

Come touch the softness of these perky petals.
Come make believe this prairie never dies.

Eve, Banished, Sunbathes

Today, I let my body drown in daylight.
All morning and all afternoon it filled
every crevice of my body, nostrils,
mouth agape, the helix of my ear.

I'm trying to appreciate the small
things now—the rays, streaming through
the clouds reminding me of all the days
I've lost, the serenades of Mourning Doves
that will soon silence as the season fades,
the cool shade of a passing puff of cloud,
the aftertaste of Eden on my tongue,
even the hints of pain, the tender aches,
the body's slow unraveling with time.

The sun knows to be gentle, takes her time
darkening my skin as hours pass
from gardenia to sandhill dust

to acorn-hued. The darkening comes
slow, unstoppable. The sky above me
reddens. It won't be long. My sunglasses
slip off.

May Day, During a Pandemic

Look at what this season's done coughed up:
groves and groves of wildflowers fading
into the past like memories, like fear.
The hoards of prairie phlox, still breathlessly

perse, hang on to life. Catalpa trees
shed their ashen petals, but they linger
on the ground, becoming history,
their pollen floating in the exhalation

of the day. The west winds wheeze and bring
the scent of soot, an augury perhaps?
Sunflowers tower over swathes of grass—
their buds shut in for now and casting shadows

as the sun, that fever in the sky,
slides into afternoon. But soon, they'll open
like our country will and peek their faces
to the world, the pandemonium

of sweat bees, hoverflies, funereal
dusky wings, and even long-nosed bats,
all eager to get back to work again—
spreading the essence of this dying spring.

Hunger

I didn't see you standing there—outside
the dark and desolate café tonight,
smoking the butt of someone's cigarette

as I parked my car beneath the streetlamp.
I only saw the orange glow of ashes
gathering at the tip, the hazy outline

of your rugged mane, the bulky jacket
hanging from your frame like skin. I thought
you might be just a shadow, but I knew

that you were real when I heard your howl
above the distant sounds of whooshing cars.
Hey there, sexy, how are you tonight?

And suddenly, I lost what makes me human.
So did you. Why did you have to speak?
I assumed the posture of a doe:

scut in the air and running for her life,
two downturned eyes the size of hunters' moons.
I wish I'd had a moment just to think,

not to react and turn into a beast
made to be devoured by another.
Maybe you saw the sadness in my eyes

and wanted me to feel beautiful.
Maybe you simply needed to be seen.
Maybe you were hungry for some bread,

or something else. To me, it didn't matter.
You lit the wick of fear within my bones.
It raged. I hurried into the café,

ordered my salad, trying to forget
what it's like to be another's prey.
I knew that you were gazing through the window—

at me or my plate? I couldn't tell.
We shared this meal of emptiness together—
my heart banged in my chest with every bite

as you watched me while standing by my car.
Probably, you're harmless—just a man
down on his luck, out in the cold, and lonely;

probably, I'm everything that's wrong
with this world—the kind of woman who
can only see the predator in you,

who can't let go of yesterday, the last
vestigial of fear beneath the surface
of my skin that burns and burns and burns.

What a cruel world we've all created—
where compassion is a luxury,
where fear and hunger seem to conquer all,

where seeing you as human is a risk
that I can't take tonight. I'm but a rabbit,
holed up in the safety of her burrow,

and you're locked in the role of timber wolf,
nose to the ground, awaiting my emergence
into the open fields of the night,

starving for something I can never give.

The Body, Before

Notice the geography of freedom—
this open prairie made of flesh, the slow
swoop of the back's small, curvature of skull,
the belly's subtle knoll. The mirror shows
this vista of my body and I gaze,
try to commit this scene to memory
like a valley filled with Black-eyed Susans
in April, touch this land of milk and honey
before the fall, my exile from myself.

The cold ink on my flesh. The thick black mark.
He draws a border on my body, says:
This is where I'll cut you.
But I hear:
separate skin from skin, flesh from flesh,
bone from bone. Even with the bridge
of sutures, healing scab, the growth of vessels
carrying my blood across this border,
this scar defines the woman I am now.

Holy Land

The sun descends in power as the clouds
slip into their golden robes. It's spring—
a blooming bush of serviceberry shrouds
the barbed-wire fence, its thorny branches
cling to the steel, its alabaster petals
grate against the edge of paradise.
Inside the fence, no wildflower settles
its roots into the soil of sacrifice
where the sacred hooves will snuff them out.
The Brahmans graze off in the distance, hidden,
awaiting the fate of everything devout.
On the pasture, morning dewdrops glisten.
This lovely landscape filled with verdant hills
holds up a sky as green as dollar bills.

Tangles

Every day I wake to this: a pit
of tangled hair, a labyrinth, an ember,
and a shelter all at once, a rhumba
of prairie king snakes slumbering, their
eyes peeled, gazing like a pair of die.

I grab the brush. It hisses, knows its worth—
this feral mop-top made of wilderness.

Some days it wants to frame my face in strength,
a lion's mane, a symbol that this woman's
got better things to do than tame her hair.

Some days it wants to hang down like a rope,
tied in a ponytail and dangling
for invited paramours to climb.

It remembers history—the battles
it always won of split ends, tugs, and curses
flung from mother's spit to daughter's snarls
for centuries, the painful yank of bullies
on the raucous playgrounds of our lives,
being chopped off, faded, bobbed, and pixied.

These tresses know what lies between the strands,
what hides atop the nape, and like Delilah,
the power of a pair of snipping shears.

But it also knows it always grows again—
a meadow overrun with dandelions
every spring, or it can be a nest
for sparrows, mockingbirds, or even falcons.
Some have said that tangled hair is sin,
serpent, and temptation. Nothing scares
this head of tangled hair. There's something deep
within these roots, the follicle, the psyche
that keeps it wild, growing, and persisting,
this daedal wonder made of mystery,

this crown I wear each night when I untie
the bun and let it fall, a flood of pleasure,
strength, and joy that rushes down my spine.

Flo and I Hike along the Platte

I'm trying to enjoy the burr oak's golds,
 the maple's reds, but God, these cramps are Hell—

ruining this afternoon just like
 so many pairs of panties, bedsheets, nights

that could have broken into blossom if
 it wasn't always autumn in my life.

I want to hike without abandon, see
 the pirouetting of vermillion

foliage splashing into flowing streams
 that whisk them deeper through the scarlet woods

where deer tracks slip into the gully's mud.
 I want to watch these torrents flush this forest

of its memories, its fallen leaves,
 witness how a season of debris

empties at the mouth into the Platte.
 I want to feel the magic of this body,

how it makes room within the womb
 to bloom again come March, the blossoms

now nothing but a feeling underneath
 the surface of this forest's sodden skin.

I know the sanguine leaves give birth to spring,
 but my lady parts are hurting like a bitch.

How to Love in Brush Country

This world will teach you how to bare your teeth
in order to survive. It teaches you
to callous, harden-up your face, your heart
in the midst of all this heat and death.

But las tunas taught me how to love—
on the roadside blooming mauve and deep
against a landscape drenched in sepia.
They hold their sweetness in their regal crown,
the only taste of sweet for miles and miles.

You have to pluck las tunas with a courage
of naivety, a little luck,
a brave stupidity, a sacred thirst.

To love a prickly pear you must forget
all you've learned about devouring—
you can't just sink your teeth into this flesh
like an apple's, spitting out the seeds.
This isn't Eden. It's the borderlands
in the dogged days of summer, August
where your hunger and your shame don't matter.

To love las tunas you must trust she'll shed
sus espinas like an attitude,
her thickest skin like work boots at the end
of a workday, and a simple swipe
can undress that golden orb that glistens
like a secret underneath the sun,
cool against your open, sweating palm.
To love las tunas means to let it go,
to soften in the face of fruit you know
can skewer you with spikes. You must forget
your teeth, become all lips and tongue and throat,
to swallow everything—the seeds, the flesh.
To love las tunas, you become a child
sticky-faced and smiling, satisfied,
leaving bits of sweetness for the birds.

Self Portrait as a Coppice of Bluebonnets

Tourists flock to see the wildflowers
blooming every April here in Brenham—
fuchsia primrose jeweled in morning's showers,
blankets of firewheels, winecups brimmed with heaven.
Bluebonnet splendor crests before their eyes
in a dazzling display of spring
that makes the fields bluer than the skies
above. The season's paramours all bring

their cameras, snap some selfies. April dulls
to August's brown. The tourists empty out;
no one comes to photograph the hulls
of beauty left behind, the face of drought,
the strangling grip of heat, the lashing gust
she weathers, tucking seeds beneath her dust.

Self Portrait as a Ghost Town

A century ago, I felt alive—
the bustle of a busy afternoon
in the town square, lovers calling out
to one another from their balconies,
gardens tended with the utmost care.

Sometimes I miss those busy days. Today,
I am a crossroads for the tumbleweeds.

The crumbled ruins of an ancient schoolhouse
that once held children in its arms of bricks
lay silent, burdened only by the sky.

The roofs gave in, collapsing one by one.
The shattered glass of windows form mosaics,
creating bursts of luster in the rubble.

The empty oil wells creek as wind blows through.

As the years go by, I've let it go
to Hell—the ryegrass and the wild oats
reclaim this swathe of dust like scabs that cover
a gaping wound that never healed quite right.

Come sit with me and learn to see the beauty
in this brokenness. A blazing sun
sets upon these hollowed bones of buildings
returning to the earth with dignity, brimming
with humus, ash, and honeysuckle.

Self Portrait as a Spent Field

I'm tired, Lord. This sanguine sky of blood.
This rusted pile of bones. This sable spirit
with sunken eyes, a worn-out bindle, hooves
becoming earth again. This soil of skin
is sick from nourishing the rows and rows
of sorghum, soybeans, corn with roots that suck
this body dry of everything it is.

I remember, as a child, these acres
wild with hawthorn trees and thickets full
of buttonbushes hiding prairie rattlers
from his boot, the scythe, the harvester's
blade. Those days have slipped like fallow earth
through my fingers: spent. I lie here now,

spritzed with fertilizer like perfume
a dusting of miasma on my surface,
in hope that it will keep me green forever.

Redbuds in a Churchyard

The prairie larkspurs bow their heavy heads.
A mantis folds its arms, awaits the coming
of the rain that brings the damsel flies
to life again. A woodpecker impales

a pine tree and its tapping fills the quiet
of the morning. Golden petals hang
from the branches of a honey locust—
a beautiful temptation crowned with thorns.

But there's one sight that stands out most of all:
A Judas tree in bloom, its sanguine blossoms
too much for it to bear this Easter morning.
You see it on your way to church and smile

at the grandeur of this April dawn.
This is what you whisper to yourself—
How lovely are those redbuds when in bloom,
glacing but the surface of this story.

Eve, Quarantined

Is this how she felt millennia
ago while sheltering in Eden's refuge?

Like her, I want for nothing in this place.
My cupboard's filled with bags of rice and beans.
My freezer's stocked with chicken, beef, and pork.
The bedroom blooms with pleasure like a garden.

The only thing that's missing is the sun—
red like apples, cherries, pomegranates
setting against the backdrop of a city
that's now a ghost town. Standing in her garden,

naked, did she gaze beyond the walls
of her home, like I do every dusk,
looking out the window, smudging it
with her palms, and weep for what she misses?

This fragile flesh, these fragile bones, be damned.
Mortality and paradise be damned.

Is this the ache she felt within her heart
to get back to the toil of the living?

Summers of Lightning Bugs

Once, I loved you like a firefly—
remember how they used to make the fields

effulgent like the midnight sky once was?
When this was open fields and the heart

grew wild like the prairie? Do you remember
how each year those lightning bugs returned?

Like spring, the cricket's song, and wild pigeons.
How their lightshow made of everything

that moves our bodies lit this backyard up?
And one by one, some darkness snuffed the fire—

little mistakes like leaving porchlights on,
the city's growing glow, the giant flares,

those blazing elephants we can't ignore
in the onyx skies that are our lives.

Now, it's night again. It's summer, too.
Now I'm sipping bourbon on the porch

gazing into fields of emptiness,
wondering what mountains I must move

to make those lightning bugs return to us.

Beekeeper's Aubade

My love, I know that hives, like hearts, collapse.
This feeling comes most often in the fall
as I'm awoken by the morning's chill
and the horizon wears the hue of blood.

The workers keep the colony alive
with a grain of insect faith that soon
this prairie will explode again with clovers
like it used to years ago. But no,

the days of wild goldenrod have passed.
The workers visit dandelions, taste
neonics on their blooms. They feel the chew
of vampire mites that suck what little succor

the planet offers. One day, a worker bee
will just give up. She'll realize her wings
are too deformed, her viral load too high,
her spirit given out. She'll make a final

pearl of precious honey for her queen,
cap the brood, and fly away without
so much as a goodbye, and then she'll die.
Her leaving is the sweetest kind of mercy—

the queen, her belly full, may yet survive,
slumbering in a sea of gold, her heart
oblivious and blissful as she makes
clutch after clutch of eggs in preparation

for the future that may never come.
I turn over in the bed and gaze
at your honeyed smile, your eyelashes
dusted still with sleep. But someone needs

to tend the bees this morning, so I rise,
dress in haste, and don my ivory veil.
I'll leave a pot of coffee for you, love,
and head into the frost to check the brood.

Her Apocalypse

I think this is how our world will end:
a mother, finished with the giving season,
feels the coming warming of her body.

Rivers of sweat begin to swell and drown
what used to be the nesting place of us.
Icecaps sag into the rising seas.
Hurricanes of grief and joy make landfall
rocking the body's shores. A trembling
beneath the surface stirs the transformation—

Red knots refuse to don their breeding plumage,
kaleidoscopes of golden monarchs thin
leaving bald spots in the ecosystem,
the blooms of wild sage each March no longer
overflow like blood across the prairie.
They fade to but a trickle, then they cease.

This is how it ends, no glorious
fanfare but a quiet revelation
in her bones that this is it—the season's done.
Our mother gazes at the stars and wonders
what new beginnings menopause will bring.

ACKNOWLEDGMENTS

The following poems have been previously published:

"My Grandma Creates the Earth," *New Texas*

"Lupinis Texanis," *Texas Poetry Calendar*

"Katy Prairie, May," *San Pedro River Review*

"Eve, Banished, Sunbathes," and "The Body, Before," *Mezzo Cammin: A Journal of Formalist Poetry by Women*

"Self Portrait as a Coppice of Bluebonnets," *Green Hills Literary Lantern*

"Self Portrait as a Ghost Town," *Switchgrass Review*

"What Cassandra Knew," *Poetry South*

"Hunger," *Tipton Poetry Review*

"Beekeeper's Aubade," *Summerset Review*

ABOUT THE AUTHOR

About a year ago, Katherine Hoerth moved to Nebraska from Texas; her poems chronicle the experience of adjusting to life on the Great Plains amid the isolation and uncertainty of the COVID-19 pandemic. The term "prairie madness" feels, Hoerth observes, particularly fitting as it was once used to describe the "madness" of women pioneers of Nebraska and Kansas who endured extreme isolation.

Hoerth is an assistant professor of English at Lamar University and editor of Lamar University Literary Press. Her work has been published in journals such as *The Georgia Review*, *Pleiades*, and *Valparaiso Review*. Katherine received a developmental leave award and is working on a book about the frontier, feminism, and eco-poetics in Omaha, Nebraska. Her collaborative poetry collection, *Borderland Mujeres*, is forthcoming from Stephen F. Austin State University Press, and her *Flare Stacks in Full Bloom* is forthcoming from Texas Review Press. She is a member of the Texas Institute of Letters, and in 2015 she won the Helen C. Smith Prize for the best book of poetry in Texas.

ABOUT THE PRESS

North Dakota State University Press (NDSU Press) exists to stimulate and coordinate interdisciplinary regional scholarship. These regions include the Red River Valley, the state of North Dakota, the plains of North America (comprising both the Great Plains of the United States and the prairies of Canada), and comparable regions of other continents.

Since 2016, NDSU Press has offered experiential learning opportunities for students interested in the history, practice, and business of publishing. We congratulate Dr. Suzzanne Kelley and the Introduction to Publishing class of fall 2021 for their outstanding accomplishment in this limited edition letterpress print production of Katherine Hoerth's Prairie Madness, winner of the 2021 Poetry of the Plains and Prairies Award.

We thank Allan Burke, of Linton, ND, for his unflagging assistance, guidance, and expertise in making our letterpress activities and publications possible.

The interior pages of *Prairie Madness* are hand letterpress printed on 32# Tortilla Southworth Naturals Paper using a Chandler & Price (1800s) and a Heidelberg (1930s) press. Each page is folded, assembled, stitched, and trimmed on site at The Braddock News Letterpress Museum in Braddock, ND. The covers are hand letterpress printed on 67# Tan Exact Vellum Bristol Premium Cardstock with a Chandler & Price press at The Hunter Times, located in West Fargo at The Hunter Times Museum, Bonanzaville. The inserts are 27# Tinted Vellum Paper.

The 2021 Introduction to Publishing Class

[left to right] Erin L. Tamillo, Dr. Kyle Vanderburg, Dr. Suzzanne Kelley, Allan Burke, Oliver West Sime

[left to right] Sarah Beck, Ryan Pedersen

Not Pictured: Sam Anderson, Tori Layne Eiss, N.J. Hansen, Tatum L. Hoff, Jack T. Monson, and Hannah-Ruth Slater.

ABOUT THE POETRY OF THE PLAINS & PRAIRIES AWARD

Our chapbook publication series began in 2016 with a collection of poetry, *Land of Sunlit Ice*, by Larry Woiwode, Poet Laureate of North Dakota. Students in the NDSU Intro to Publishing course hand stenciled each cover with four colors of paint, and hand letterpressed, assembled, stitched, trimmed, and numbered each of more than two hundred copies. The project was such a success that the course instructor, Dr. Suzzanne Kelley, sought a second chapbook collection, *Thunderbird*, by Denise K. Lajimodiere. Both of these first collections sold out.

By the time of the third publication, the series developed a name, now known as the Poetry of the Plains & Prairies (POPP) Award. Each year, through a national solicitation process, poets from anywhere can submit poetry collections of no more than forty pages for the competitive selection process. Authors from Texas to Maine and closer environs have submitted works for consideration. The collection you now hold is the sixth in our chapbook series and winner of the 2021 POPP Award. Winners of the annual competition are awarded our standard publishing contract, ten complimentary copies, and national distribution. The open submissions period for the annual competition is from January 17 to March 17. There is no fee to enter.

1. 2016: *Land of Sunlit Ice*, Larry Woiwode (North Dakota)
2. 2017: *Thunderbird*, Denise K. Lajimodiere (North Dakota)
3. 2018: *Destiny Manifested*, Bonnie Larson Staiger (North Dakota)
4. 2019: *Harvest Widows*, Nick Bertelson (Iowa)
5. 2020: *A Muddy Kind of Love*, Carolyn Dahl (Texas)
6. 2021: *Prairie Madness*, Katherine Hoerth (Nebraska)